extreme sports

mad moose press

Managing Editors: Simon Melhuish and Emma Craven
Author and Series Editor: Lee Linford
Design: Alan Shiner

Designed and compiled by
Mad Moose Press
for
Lagoon Books
PO Box 311, KT2 5QW, UK
PO Box 990676, Boston, MA 02199, USA

ISBN: 1-904139-00-0

www.madmoosepress.com
www.lagoongames.com

extreme sports

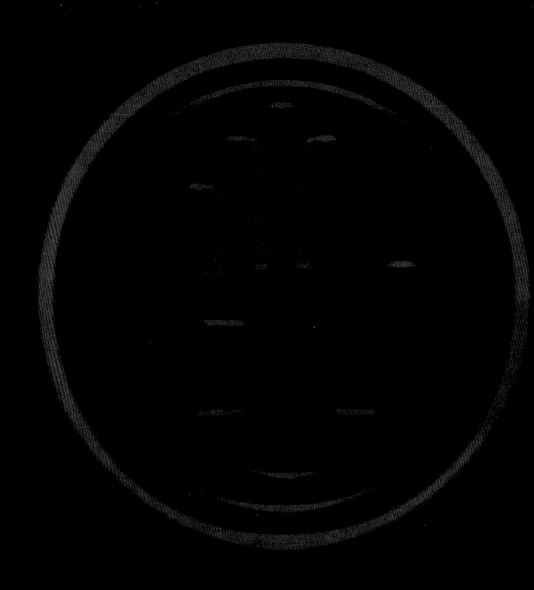

Adrenalin - a dangerous addiction.

Everyone's searching for the ultimate
buzz; for some it's a way of life, for
others a regular fix of armchair
escapism.

Advanced technology means bigger
rushes, less risk. But no matter how
advanced your equipment, extreme
sports are essentially just that -
extreme.

Whether you prefer jumping from planes
or off cliffs, shooting rapids (with or
without a boat) or riding forty foot
waves, take a breather and flick through
this book for some fresh inspiration for
your next adventure.

catch some
mountain air

white-out • wipe-out

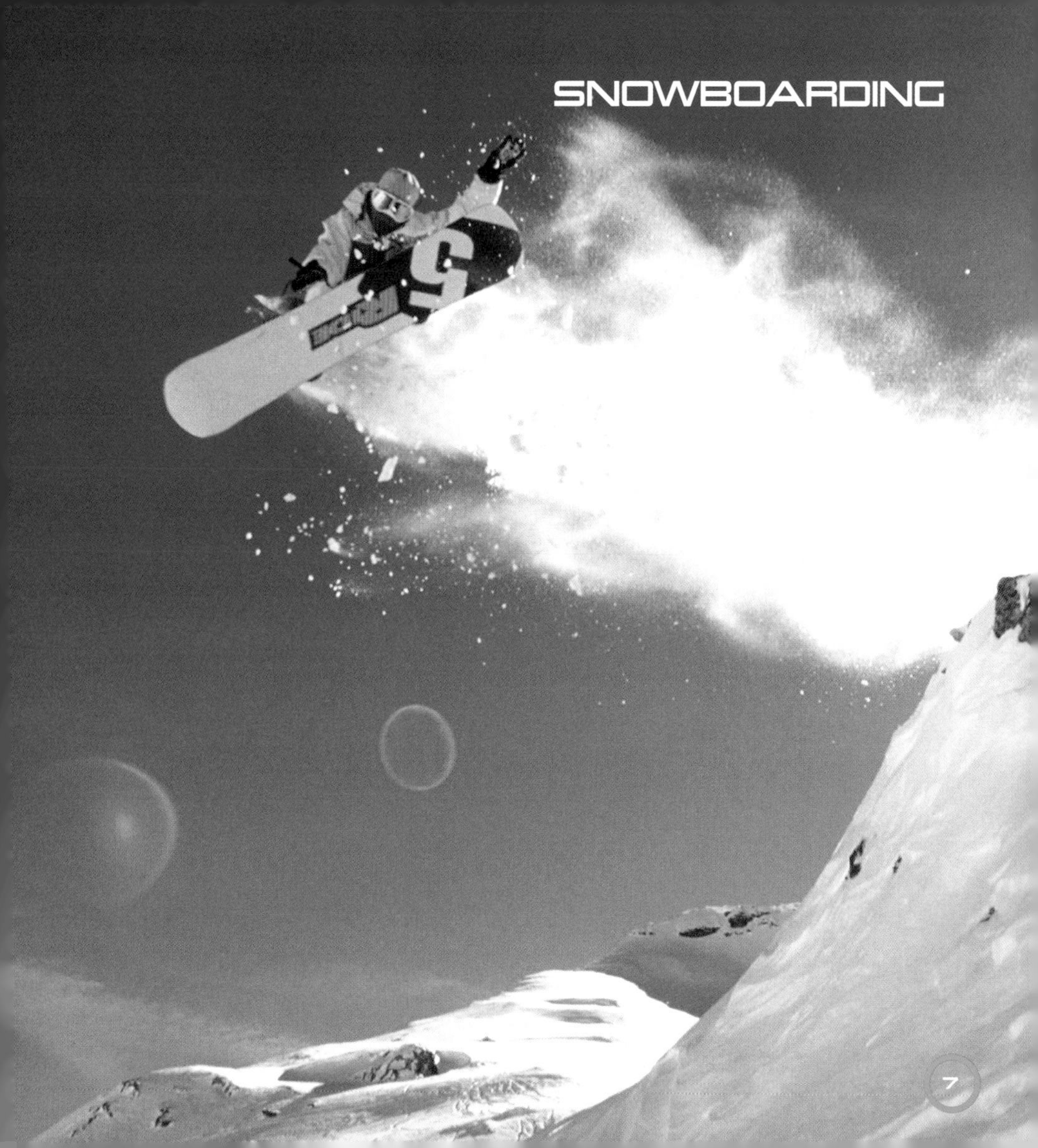

all style • no style • freestyle

off-piste • off a cliff

catch some air • catch your breath

danger rating ●●●●●●●○○

sky-scrapers

total gravity feed

B. A. S. E.

Building. Antenna. Span. Earth.

Blatantly. Awaiting. Sanity. Evaluation.

danger rating ●●●●●●●●●●

water.

Fall.

go to the edge then keep on going

15

still waters run deep.

shallow waters run rapids.

vertical waters run on high octane.

danger rating ●●●●●●●●

cruise

control

life's a breeze · life's a force 9 gale

adrenalin rush ●●●●●●●●●

high tide • low tide • rip tide

go where the mood takes you

go where the wind takes you

get a grip

up the slippery slope

untouched, pristine, ever different.

icicles the size of bicycles.

determination: the only constant.

depth
charge

breathe deep • go deep

propel through the watery darkness.

downward thrust, fluid motion.

heartbeat like a slowing clock,

air supply in a single breath.

going

nowhere

Fast

make molehills out of mountains

adrenalin rush ○○○○○○○○○○

mud, rock, river, ice.

always take the path

of greatest resistance.

danger rating ●●●●●●●

cloud nine

collision

course

suspended animation

soar like an eagle,

float like a feather;

launch yourself onto

a higher plane;

feet to terra firma.

danger rating ◉◉◉◉◉◉◉○◖

man over

board

hands off the deck

adrenalin rush ●●●●●●●●○

heelflip indy 540.

popshuvit nosegrind.

nollie flip backside tailslide.

no need to understand it,

just get on and do it.

this is your

wake-up call

make your own waves.

ride them your own way.

vertically

challenged

another hangover from hell

steady progress,

heady heights.

serious action

in ultra slow motion.

danger rating ⬤⬤⬤⬤⬤⬤⬤⬤⬤

high and dry

rule the airwaves

adrenalin rush ○○○○○○○○○

ozone • dropzone • in the zone

whatever the conditions,

the surf is always up

danger rating ●●●●●●●●●

rapid

descent

through hell and high water

WHITE-WATER RAFTING

gentle trickle to raging torrent,

a new buzz around every bend.

all in the same boat;

aiming to stay that way.

danger rating ●●●●●●●●●

snowstorm

trigger the adrenalin avalanche

trailblazer, ice-breaker, powder explosion.

cut your own path

through the bleached-out wilderness

danger rating ●●●●●●●●●

mexican

wave

breaks · no brakes

adrenalin rush ● ● ● ● ● ● ● ● ●

run with white horses,

ride with the monster.

enter the green room,

touch the face of danger.

danger rating ●●●●●●●

cruising at 25,000 Feet

where yetis fear to tread

scale new heights,

reach new peaks;

take a different view

from the roof of the world.

danger rating ●●●●●●●●●●

saddle soar

jump and grind

go gonzo, get sick.

a full phat diet;

steering clear of potato chips.

danger rating ●●●●●●●●

down. under.

one colossal drop in the ocean

extreme elevation

to deep blue sea.

a bird, a plane,

a one man submersible.

danger rating ●●●●●●●●

dry ice

just deserts

45° in forty five degrees.

fuel the euphoria

in the fiery furnace.

danger rating ●●●●●●●○

body. rock.

white water without the raft

precipice, ravine, cascade.

follow the river's course,

wherever it may flow.

danger rating ●●●●●●●●◖

power

surge

switch on the current

adrenalin rush ●●●●●●●●●

downwind • upwind • crosswind

harness nature's power;

achieve air superiority.

danger rating ●●●●●●●○

soak up the atmosphere

the ultimate 3 minute mile

adrenalin rush ●●●●●●●●●●

glide with the thermals,

drop like a rock.

downforce. updraft. groundrush.

live life at terminal velocity

danger rating ●●●●●●●●

If you're thinking extreme, start surfing.

Extreme sports
www.expn.go.com
www.pie.com
www.boarding.com
www.mountainzone.com
www.transworldmatrix.com
www.waxed.com
www.extremesports.with1click.com

Snowboarding
www.worldsnowboardguide.com
www.snowboarding.com
www.boardtheworld.com

Base jumping
www.theipbc.com
www.ground-rush.com/base.htm
www.basejumping.co.uk

White-water kayaking
www.worldkayak.com
www.whitewater.org

Windsurfing
www.windsurfer.com
www.iwindsurf.com

Rock climbing & ice climbing
www.rockandice.com
www.climbing.com

Free diving
www.freediver.net

Mountain biking
www.dirtworld.com
www.imba.com

Paragliding
www.bigairparagliding.com
www.paragliding.org
www.bhpa.co.uk

Skateboarding
www.skateboarding.com
www.skateboardeurope.com

Wakeboarding
www.wakeboarder.com
www.wakeworld.com

Sky surfing
www.ground-rush.com/surf.htm

White-water rafting
www.raftinfo.com
www.riverrafting.com

Free skiing
www.freeskiers.org
www.3do.com/freeski

Surfing
www.surfinfo.com
www.swell.com
www.worldsurfers.com
www.ripcurl.com

Mountaineering
www.thebmc.co.uk
www.americanalpineclub.org
www.mountaineers.net

BMXing
www.bmxonline.com

Cliff diving
www.procliffdiving.com

Sandboarding
www.sandboard.com
www.duneriders.org

Canyoning
www.canyoneering.net
www.hikercentral.com/canyoning

Kite surfing
www.oceanextreme.com
www. kitesurfing.org
www.kitesurfnews.com

Skydiving
www.uspa.org
www.ground-rush.com